PAY

THE

PRICE

JACK D. KNUTSON

Published in the United States of America

ISBN: 978-0-578-91594-4

Contents

Introduction

We all spend many years in formal education, preparing for our future. There seems to be little time spent preparing how to live!

It has been said that knowledge is organized fact—wisdom is organized life!

Many people grow up with the good fortune to have learned much of what follows in our little book, whether through an enlightened mentor or simply a well-intentioned family member. However, I believe that many have not had this mentoring and coaching so critical to an understanding of life's essential demands.

I had an old friend who used to say, "If you don't know where you are going, any old road will get you there." His other saying was "If you don't know where you are going, you might end up somewhere else." I suppose that is typically true! It is our ardent hope to lend direction.

We will address the imperativeness of goal setting, of having a vision, a purpose, a direction. A goal or dream is simply that. We must follow it with action. Nothing typically happens without WORK, dedicated hard work. The harder we work, the luckier we get. When the inevitable head winds blow, the adversities of life, we must stay the course— perseverance. We will discuss many other virtues and qualities of character that lend themselves to a balanced and effective lifestyle.

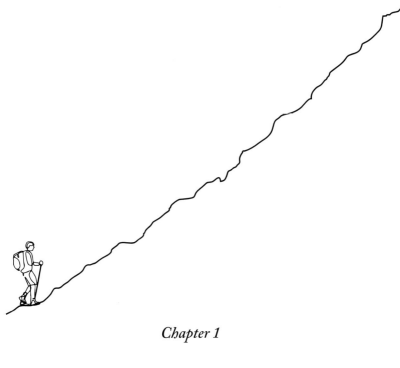

Chapter 1

On Goals

"Goals help us achieve our highest potential."

We must have definite, clearly set goals, or we will not maximize the potential that lies within us. A person without a goal is like a ship without a rudder. You will end up washed ashore.

Many people make the same mistake and reap only a small fraction of the harvest life has to offer. They blindly follow the crowd aimlessly wandering. They follow methods and procedures for no other reason than, "It's always been done that way."

Do people who don't succeed plan to fail? No, they simply fail to plan. The purpose of planning is to enhance accomplishment and success in your life. It allows you to do more for yourself and others. There exists a thought that unless we are moving onwards and upwards towards an objective, a goal, we will falter and fail.

With definite goals you release your own power, and things start happening. In order for goals to be effective they need to be big, because it takes a big goal to create the excitement necessary for accomplishment. There is no excitement in keeping up with somebody else. The excitement comes when you do your best, which you can only do with the proper goals. If you want to sleep like a baby, do your best today. Make no small plans, for they cannot stir men's souls.

You can only go as far as you can see at the time. Once you follow that path as long as you can, you will often find you can now look up and see a little bit further ahead. In this way we make steady progress toward a worthwhile objective—this by itself helps give your life additional meaning.

So, take control of your life! When you stop to set goals and think about what you want, you break out and start living a life that you have consciously decided upon. Instead of letting others tell you what to do, you proactively take charge and think about what you want for yourself!

Goals propel us to take action and accomplish more. Things are created twice: first in the mind, then in reality. Without a goal, plan, or dream, is it possible to feel in control? When you set goals, you ignite the first step in making your dreams happen.

Having a general direction, or a tentative goal, is not enough. We may only get tentative results. Take dead aim to get precise results.

Having goals makes us accountable. Put them in writing and make a specific, established deadline. We are four times more likely to achieve something if we put it in writing. Writing helps ensure we process things. Seeing them in writing gives us a visual reinforcement. Post those dreams and plans where you will see them daily. Eventually they will be embedded in your subconscious and you can live them. Our subconscious directs our conscious mind, which drives us to get what we want. Rather than just talk, become obligated. Goals help motivate us and give us something to strive for. If we have nothing to strive for, we become aimless and listless. Your goals are your rainbow to reach for, to pull you out of the storm.

Goals help you achieve your highest potential. By setting goals, you project yourself towards a target and propel yourself towards new heights. Goals ensure you get the best out of life!

Why do those with goals succeed in life, and those without them fail? Because "we become what we think about." The great teachers agree on one point, the key to success and the key to failure is this, "We become what we think about."

The great Roman Emperor Marcus Aurelius said, "A man's life is what his thoughts make it." William James said, "The greatest discovery of my generation is that human beings can alter their lives by altering their attitudes of mind."

Plant your goal in your mind. What is it you want? What is it? Plant the seed in your mind, nurture and care for it, work steadily towards your goal, and it will inevitably come to pass.

Goals give us direction and purpose. Now couple it with work and faith.

Chapter 2

On Work

"Some people dream of success—others wake up and work hard for it!"

The only place success comes before work is in the dictionary! Most of us must have gainful employment to get along in life. We need to earn an income for the simple sheer necessities of life: food, clothing, and shelter. However, while work is necessary for most, it also is a great source of self-worth, satisfaction, and accomplishment.

Typically, we are more gratified in a vocation that interests us, even if it does not pay as much as another career. If we are fortunate to have a job that we are passionate about, life can be more fun and rewarding and the compensation will follow.

By simple definition, a job is a job, a task! There will be times of enjoyment as well as struggle. We shall not take our vocations lightly—obviously, they are a major part of our lives. Remember the adage "school is never out for the pro." Stay interested and focused on your career. Remember the best antidote for being average is to pay the price.

Again, pay the price. Go the extra mile. We are usually rewarded in proportion to our efforts. Rather than pitying our lot in life, why not try to be the best at what we do? The coolest example I ever saw was when I was changing planes in Detroit, Michigan a few years ago. As I walked out of my plane heading to another gate, I walked past a custodian collecting trash. He was singing, and singing well. I stopped and chatted with him. He had been an entertainer for a bit in his early years. I explained how wonderful it was to see him singing away as he dumped trash. I asked him if I could video him a little. Of course, he was happy to do that. Part of the way through, I put my arm on his shoulder and we sang together. I left that man inspired and enriched. Now that was a case of making lemonade out of a lemon. Doing a job, no matter what, with a decent attitude and conscientiousness will pay dividends. The choice is ours! Grumble and look like sour lemons, or dance a little in the rain.

Hard work builds character. We live in an era of instant gratification. If the accomplishment is hard, we often lose interest or give up. But hard work builds character. We learn discipline and focus. Don't be a quitter. Quitting is easy. Giving up is easy. But easy never builds character. Success isn't the greatest reward for hard work. Character is more important than success. And hard work builds character.

Hard work always accomplishes something—it always gets results. Some people dream of success… while others wake up and work hard for it. Hard work draws attention. If you want to get noticed, work hard, and you will stand out. It doesn't matter how talented you are, or what you are called to do—do it with passion. Put your heart into it. Hard work brings new opportunity, it opens doors. The harder we work, the luckier we get. Most simply complain of no luck. Hard work attracts opportunity. Thomas Edison said, "Opportunity is missed by most people because it is dressed in overalls and looks like work." No lasting benefit is achieved without hard work!

There are countless examples of average people who have risen to excellence in their field of endeavor. It typically is not by accident—they worked their tails off. Average accomplishment is not as challenging, but we will get average results. It usually takes an all-encompassing obsession to excel. An obsession to grow, to learn, to work, to persevere, and strive for excellence.

I am always amused when the Olympics come around. We see world-class athletes in action. We are told how hard they work, how the endless hours of practice prepared them for competition. There are times when who appears to be the superior athlete does not win their event. Often, the winner works the hardest and is the most determined.

It is almost cliché in the coaching arena to say, "Give me a coachable, determined, hardworking athlete, not simply the best all-around athlete."

It Couldn't Be Done

Somebody said that it couldn't be done,
But he with a chuckle replied
That "maybe it couldn't," but he would be one
Who wouldn't say so till he'd tried.
So he buckled right in with the trace of a grin
On his face. If he worried he hid it.
He started to sing as he tackled the thing
That couldn't be done, and he did it.

Somebody scoffed: "Oh, you'll never do that;
At least no one ever has done it";
But he took off his coat and he took off his hat,
And the first thing we knew he'd begun it.
With a lift of his chin and a bit of a grin,
Without any doubting or quiddit,
He started to sing as he tackled the thing
That couldn't be done, and he did it.

There are thousands to tell you it cannot be done,
There are thousands to prophesy failure;
There are thousands to point out to you one by one,
The dangers that wait to assail you.
But just buckle in with a bit of a grin,
Just take off your coat and go to it;
Just start in to sing as you tackle the thing
That "cannot be done," and you'll do it.
—Edgar A. Guest

Chapter 3

On Perseverance/Endurance

*"Armed with determination and
perseverance, everything is possible."*

*"Nothing in the world can take the place of persistence.
Talent will not; nothing is more common than unsuccessful
men with talent. Genius will not; unrewarded genius is
almost a proverb. Education will not; the world is full of
educated derelicts. Persistence and determination alone
are."*—Calvin Coolidge

Success has been defined as the "progressive realization of a pre-determined worthwhile goal." It seems that in order to progress, we have to persist. Talent is great, education is great, ability is great…yet all are of no value without <u>determination</u> and <u>perseverance</u>! Establish a goal or mission and remain steadfast.

Successful lives seem to have one thing in common: the trait of endurance. Success does not come without its setbacks. We must travel our journey, through good and bad. All great people have had tremendous staying power.

I know an Army Ranger from the Vietnam War. He saw a lot of action in the jungle towards the front line. He has had numerous setbacks and challenges in civilian life since then. He was diagnosed with post-traumatic stress disorder many years after being discharged. I once asked him how he had the resilience and tenacity to fight on, not giving in to despair. His answer was simple, yet profound. Just keep putting one foot ahead of the other. I am certain that was a conditioned response of our military's special forces. "One foot ahead of the other."

There are times in our lives when that is about all we can do! It may be slow, but we are moving ahead.

There is not an express elevator to the top. It is much more of a staircase. It may be slow, it may be arduous, there may be times we step backward, and times we pause. With our eyes looking to the goal, the finish line, we will stay methodical and consistent in our ascent.

Success does not necessarily mean intelligence. Intelligent people who don't apply themselves and have tenacity and persistence will usually die on the vine, never realizing their goals and dreams. These people usually give up due to a lack of perseverance. On the other hand, an individual who is not highly knowledgeable or talented but believes hard work will make him succeed puts his efforts into action, and persists, however long it takes.

Jack Canfield is the creator of the *Chicken Soup for the Soul* series. He is also a remarkable motivational speaker, professional coach, and an incredibly inspiring author who published success principles. Jack and his co-author, Mark Victor Hansen, pitched the original *Chicken Soup for the Soul* to over 130 different publishers. None of them were interested and said "No one wants to read 100 inspirational stories."

After 100 pitches, their agent dropped them as well, but they were still determined to get the book published. They never gave up and continued to persevere until their book was picked up by a small publisher in Florida.

Now there are over 250 *Chicken Soup for the Soul* books and over 500 million copies sold worldwide.

If they would have given up after the 130 publishers, we would not have their inspirational stories, nor would they have had their phenomenal success.

In conclusion, all aspects of life require perseverance. People can learn different skills, and have the knowledge and the will to work, yet without perseverance, they end up failing to achieve their ultimate goals in life. This vigorous journey is achieved by overcoming things like failures, obstacles, hurdles, and laziness, to name but a few. Therefore, with one's determination and perseverance, everything is possible.

Chapter 4

On Discipline

"Self-discipline allows us to improve daily."

Self-discipline is a major key to success. It would be very difficult to succeed in life without it.

Self-discipline helps us become a dynamic force of energy. Someone once told me the difference between a typical blocker in the NFL and a "Hall of Fame blocker" is 100,000 blocks—achieved by work and discipline. If we really want success, we have to discipline ourselves.

Self-discipline is critical to get things done. This habit makes us an achiever in our lives. It helps us remain consistent in life, and when we are consistent, we can attain our goals. Successful people discipline themselves to work and be methodical. We cultivate it as a habit, which enhances success in our lives.

Successful people have their eye on the ball—they are focused. There are many distractions in our lives. Self-discipline helps us focus on our goals. It helps us stay with the work we need to get done to achieve our goals and success. Our focus and discipline make us unstoppable. Self-discipline enhances our self-esteem and our work ethic. When we discipline ourselves, we improve our work ethic by staying with it. To reach our goals, discipline is imperative. By completing our objectives, we gain confidence. Discipline and a quiet confidence will always serve us well.

When you do something consistently, you get better by and by. Success comes when you deserve it. Self-discipline allows you to improve yourself daily.

When preparation meets opportunity, we are allowed a time to shine, a time in the sun. Discipline requires commitment. It is not a "sometimes" thing. It needs to be consistent and methodical.

If we are committed and dedicated to our goals, we are going to be successful. Be uncommon. Be that minority of people who actually make a commitment. Once you have done that, it is time to do the work. It may not be easy. Remember, work comes before success. We have to discipline ourselves, we have to start, and we must be warriors. Only then do we deserve our successes. We must keep away from distractions while in the pursuit of accomplishment. Like I tell my sons, "Be about what you are about. Be on task." If we relentlessly pursue anything, and have self-discipline, we shall not be denied!

Almost invariably, top-performers and peak-achievers are extremely disciplined. They have a routine and stick with it. The famous wide-receiver, Jerry Rice, of the San Francisco 49ers, is a classic example. He was so rigorous and disciplined about every facet of his preparation and training. For example, even how his uniform was laid out before a game. His equipment manager knew exactly how he liked it laid out and was meticulous in following Jerry's protocol. His workouts were legendary, knowing he had to be disciplined and focused to stay at his peak.

Waler Payton of the Chicago Bears, one of the top running-backs of all time, was also known for his rigorous workout and disciplined life. Very simply, people like Jerry and Walter earned their way to the top of their profession through dedication and self-discipline.

Chapter 5

On Self Responsibility

"Excuses are usually a cop-out."

Consider the concept of living a "No Excuse" life. We try to displace our responsibility in many situations by making excuses. Excuses are usually a cop-out! We are simply trying to rationalize why something did not get done, trying to shift responsibility.

Military training often involves teaching three responses: Yes, sir; No, sir; and No excuses, sir. When we accept accountability, we achieve more! By refusing excuses and embracing responsibility, we move ahead with determination and conviction. The successes brought by this attitude act as a foundation for self-respect, pride, and confidence. Responsibility fosters competence and power. Making excuses only hinders progress, while <u>accepting responsibility enhances it.</u>

We must come to realize and accept that our success or failure depends on us! It depends on our attitude and the choices we make. Let's not make an excuse, but rather a way. Accept responsibility.

It is easy to rationalize what we are doing, and why things are not getting done. Be aware of this and make no excuses. When we make a mistake, let's own it. Let's accept it, learn from it, and not repeat it. The challenge is to be problem solvers rather than excuse-makers.

Strive for the excitement and joy that self-responsibility brings when you accomplish a goal. It is a great feeling when we accept that outcomes depend on actions. Even though the decision-making process can be influenced by others, it is your decision to act or not. The way we live our lives is based on our actions. We must recognize the responsibility we bear for our own lives. To stop blaming others for our mistakes and failures. It is easy to make excuses. It is almost natural! We need a quick response. However, our best path is one of self-responsibility and action. The lasting way to growth and change is being responsible.

Self-responsibility and not finding excuses help you become your best self. We all have different definitions of success. In our quest for success and accomplishment, one of the key elements is self-responsibility. We are at the steering wheel of our lives, and we have the power to influence it. Take charge and take responsibility for your actions, good or bad, and you will start to see a change in your lives.

Taking responsibility is simply accepting that we are the only ones who can change our life for the better. No one can do it for us. We are in control, and excuses don't get results. It is easier to be a victim and blame others, or circumstances, than to accept responsibility. That only keeps us stuck in nowhere land. Taking acceptance of one's responsibility and not avoiding it, leads to accomplishment and satisfaction.

Successful leaders do not make excuses for their actions or actions gone wrong, they make things happen regardless of the situation or circumstances.

People use excuses to avoid blame. This is for things they said they were going to do but did not follow through. Excuses are usually just lies for not doing something, while the real reason was that it wasn't a priority. Things that we make a priority, we do not need to make excuses for.

Leaders are not short-sighted. They will make sacrifices in the short-term for the opportunity in order to achieve their goals.

Leaders are comfortable with failure because they have seen it, felt it, lived it, and understand it is part of the overall process. Do not avoid failure by making excuses. When leaders fail they do not make excuses, they do not blame others. Leaders know they can only improve by the admission of a mistake and correcting the error. Learning from our mistakes, taking responsibility, helps us to grow, change and move towards our goal.

Chapter 6

On Action

"Whatever you can do, or dream
you can do, begin it."
—William Hutchinson Murray

"To reach a port we must sail, sometimes
with the wind, and sometimes against it.
But we must not drift or lie at anchor."
—Oliver Wendell Holmes

Be active, not passive. Don't idly expect the good things of life to find you—go search for them. It is not enough to simply be on the right course. Get going.

There are four kinds of people:

1. Wishbone People - They wish for and long for and sigh, but don't have the get-up to try.
2. Funny Bone People - Life is a joke and levity blinds the eye—so, when accomplishment beckons, they ask sneeringly, "Why?"
3. Jawbone People - They jaw, rave and cry—long on talk but short on try.
4. Backbone People - Up and at it, they ascend the summits high, for they seek and seek, try and try.

Do not be satisfied with mediocrity. Upon awakening each morning, encourage your spirit to rise to that person you want to be and every day seek to achieve a little more of that image. Many have good intentions but not the vision to put first things first.

> *"Let your eyes look straight ahead; fix*
> *your gaze directly before you. Give careful*
> *thought to the paths for your feet and be*
> *steadfast in all your ways."*
> —Proverbs 4:25-26

The crime in life is not to not reach your goals, but rather to have none! No one is coming to save the day. The sooner you realize that most things are up to you, the sooner you will improve your life. Personal responsibility is important to improve and control your own life. Without that, what you want will pretty much remain a dream that leads to pretty much nothing in the long term. Remember the adage "If it is meant to be, it is up to me." Reading positive and helpful material can help motivate you in a world where you might be surrounded by negativity, such as 24-hour news or negative, or pessimistic people around you. It may be a good habit to read personal development books rather than watch too much troubling news. Many people, however, believe that reading will replace action. The goal is to stimulate action. Knowledge can help us avoid pitfalls and improve quickly. But it cannot replace experience. Part of the fun in life can be experiencing things, not simply reading and thinking about them.

One of the big challenges in life is to do the right thing. Not what your friends, family, and society think. Often, we have a gut feeling as to the right things. It might be as simple as getting off our backside and going for a walk or some form of exercise. Creating a habit where you take action every day and do the right thing is important to get the results you want. It helps raise and keep up your self-esteem. When we do the right thing—which may be difficult—instead of making excuses, our self-esteem goes up.

> *"Your life is not endless. Your time is one the most important things in your life. Don't waste a huge chunk of it. Start taking action towards what you really want out of life today."*
> —Henrik Edberg

Leap and the net will appear.

The Story of the Tiger and the Fox

A man was walking through a forest when he saw a crippled fox. "I wonder how it manages to feed itself?" The man thought to himself.

At that very moment, a tiger appeared, carrying its prey in its mouth. The tiger ate its fill and left what remained for the crippled fox.

"If God helps the fox, he will help me too," The man thought. He immediately went back home, shut himself up in his house and waited for God to bring him food. Nothing happened.

He lay in his bed just waiting for God to provide for him as he had provided for the fox, but the man just starved.

Just when he was becoming almost too weak to go out and work, an angel appeared. The angel said "Why did you decide to imitate the crippled fox?" "God has given you gifts to think, to reason, to hunt, to grow plants and animals. God has given you strengthen and abilities to contribute to the world. God helps those who strive, struggle and make efforts, and God does all of this while at the same time looking after the crippled foxes of the world. Now! Get out of that bed, pick up your tools and follow the way of the tiger not the way of a crippled Fox.

Now! I only have one question for you today. Which one are you, the lazy minded man who refuses to leave the comfort of his home, to strive and struggle for his livelihood, or the crippled fox or the tiger?

"Until one is committed, there is hesitancy, the chance to draw back. Concerning all acts of initiative (and creation), there is one elementary truth, the ignorance of which kills countless ideas and splendid plans: that the moment one definitely commits oneself, then Providence moves too. All sorts of things occur to help one that would never otherwise have occurred. A whole stream of events issues from the decision, raising in one's favor all manner of unforeseen incidents and meetings and material assistance, which no man could have dreamed would have come his way. Whatever you can do, or dream you can do, begin it. Boldness has genius, power, and magic in it. Begin it now.
—William Hutchinson Murray

Chapter 7

On Attitude

"The principal business of life is to enjoy it."

It has been said that life is 10% what happens to us, and 90% how we react! This makes a lot of sense when you understand that there are many situations in life we can't control.

Viktor E. Frankl, the Austrian Psychiatrist, Holocaust survivor, and Man's Search For Meaning author, was shuttled between four concentration camps in three years during World War II. After being tortured and stripped of everything by the Nazis, he came to the profound conclusion that everything could be taken from a person but the ability to choose one's attitude in any circumstances. He understood that nobody could control his attitude! They could take everything from him, but he still chose and controlled his attitude.

In life, we are either going in, in, or coming out of a catastrophe at any given moment. However, we can control our reaction, our attitude if you will, in these given situations.

Our attitude, to a surprising extent, determines our success or failure. William James, who some call the father of American psychology, said the greatest discovery of his generation was that "Human beings can alter their lives by altering their attitudes of mind." A big smile warms the heart and soul of others. Why not try to wear one? It is a great gift to others.

A positive attitude helps us cope more easily with the daily affairs of life. It brings optimism into life, and makes it easier to avoid worry and negative thinking. If you adopt a positive attitude as a way of life, it will bring constructive changes into your existence, and make you happier, brighter, and more successful. With a positive attitude, you see the bright side of life, become optimistic and expect the best to happen. It certainly is a state of mind that is well worth developing and strengthening.

A positive attitude leads to happiness and success and can change your whole life. Look on the bright side of life and your whole life becomes filled with light. This light not only affects you and the way you look at the world, but also your whole environment and the people around you. If it is strong enough, it becomes contagious. Success can be achieved faster and more easily. You can attain more happiness, more energy, greater power and strength, and the ability to motivate yourself and others. You'll encounter fewer difficulties along the way and life will smile at you.

> *"A cheerful heart is good medicine, but a crushed spirit dries up the bones."*
> —Proverbs 17:22

Happy and successful people are cheerful and hopeful and trod their paths through both good and difficulty with a smile! They neither grumble nor frown. A smile usually produces happiness! Do not wait until everything is perfect, go ahead and smile now. A joyful spirit will follow. Try smiling now! A smile is the universal language. We may not understand someone, yet we feel the warmth and welcome of a smile.

> *"Smile awhile and while you smile -*
> *another smiles, and soon there are miles*
> *and miles of smiles and life's worthwhile*
> *because you smile."*
> —Kathleen J. Edgar

And so, it is with all things. If you are not happy, act the happy man. Happiness will come later. So also, with faith. If you are in despair, act as though you believed. Faith will come afterwards.

ATTITUDE

The longer I live, the more I realize the impact of attitude of life. Attitude, to me, is more important then facts. It is more important than the past, than education, than money, than circumstances, than failures, than successes, than what other people think or say or do. It is more important than appearance, giftedness, or skill. It will make or break a company... a church... a home. The remarkable thing is we have a choice every day regarding the attitude we will embrace for that day. We cannot change our past... we cannot change the fact that people will act in a certain way. We cannot change the inevitable. The only thing we can do is play on the one string we have, and that is our attitude... I am convinced that life is 10% what happens to me and 90% how I react to it.

And so it is with you...
We are in charge of our ATTITUDES!

—Charles Swindoll

Chapter 8

On Self-Image/Self-Perception

"Our self-image contributes to our attitude."

A concept of psychology is, "We are not who we think we are, we are not what others think we are, rather, we are what we think others think we are!"

It is a looking glass-self-image. We tend to get a lot of our self-image from how others respond and treat us.

Sometimes we have to talk to ourselves. People may underestimate us or have the wrong impression. We can enhance our own self-image by telling ourselves we are better, smarter, or kinder than they perceive us to be. Don't ever let anyone tell you that you can't do something or be something. We must decide who we are and what our capacities are. Don't ever let someone determine your worth or value. Have a pep talk with yourself if necessary. We are what we think we are. "As a man thinketh, so he is, as he continues to think, so shall he remain," says James Allen.

Confidence starts with believing in yourself. It allows us to perform our best, with less doubt. We don't acquire confidence without working at it. We must work at it with tenacity and determination. Slowly we develop mental toughness and start to see ourselves as winners. We think like winners. We have pummeled our bodies and minds and expect to win. You see, we must "pay the price" to grow in confidence. As we grow in confidence, we expect to win. We have to earn the right to succeed—by hard work and a dogged determination. A single-minded dogged determination.

In a survey conducted by the American Psychological Association, adults rated the most important factor in achieving a positive self-image and well-being is self-esteem. Without a positive sense of self-esteem, it is very difficult to maintain a positive self-image. Positive self-esteem is something that is developed, learned, and experienced through simple practice, work, and discipline. The path to a good self-image is developing a way to feel good about yourself on a consistent basis. We strive to do those right things, whatever they may be. Discipline allows for and increases our self-esteem, which leads to that healthy self-image.

> *"Whether you think you can, or you think you can't,*
> *you are right."*
> —Henry Ford

Read success stories, biographies, and autobiographies of people who rose to prominence and fame. It is always inspiring to hear of big success, especially when they rose from obscurity. Listen to motivational speakers and teachers. Be a sponge at absorbing high-achieving, successful people. If you want to feel good about yourself, do something for others. Do it with no intention of compensation. It has to be voluntary and from your heart. It truly is in helping and serving that we receive. A simple smile to others can have tremendous uplift.

I was recently in a grocery store and happened to notice an elderly lady. She was dressed wonderfully and had just the right amount of makeup. I really wanted to tell her how great she looked. I felt she might have got all prettied up just to feel good and go shopping. However, I felt a little strange about saying anything. Later, as I was about to leave, I saw her again. I pounced to action and told her how nice she looked. You should have seen the radiance jump out. She gave me the biggest smile and thanked me. I hoped it made her day—it sure made me feel good!

Guard your friends and associates. "Birds of a feather, flock together." Seek out people of good character who look on the bright side of life. The benefits will be enormous. Make a list of both your good qualities and your past successes. Remind yourself of your worth!

Chapter 9

On Positive Self-Expectancy/Faith

"Winners expect to win!"

According to your faith, be it unto you!

As James Allen so aptly put it, "As he (a man) thinks, so he is; as he continues to think, so he remains."

Life is a self-fulfilling prophecy. We usually get what we expect. The body tries to accomplish what the mind feeds it, so program your mind for wellness, happiness, success, and accomplishment.

We must control our mind in the midst of adversity. We have to be vigilante to maintain a positive self-expectancy. We are reminded of the quote from author and activist Helen Keller, "keep your face to the sun and you will never see the shadows." Keep your eye on the goal moving forward, not seeing the shadows of distraction.

I am sometimes annoyed when I greet a friend and say, "How are you doing?" and they respond, "I'm hanging in there!" Really, is that all we can do—hang in there? We do hit rough times, and that is about all we feel. But let's not make it a pattern. The opposite that salespeople are often taught is "I am doing great!" Which one do we enjoy meeting, which one would we prefer to be? Another comment we hear is, "Well, with my luck it will never work." I think most of us would rather spend time with someone a little more optimistic, hopeful, someone who has a positive expectancy that things will work out well. Bring the challenge, life always has plenty. I am a fighter. I will do my best. I expect to prevail.

People with negative perspectives and cynical attitudes are overwhelmed with their issues. They obsess and waste time fretting and self-pitying their challenges. Winners and positive people quickly accept their challenges and seek a solution. There are times to simply embrace the problem. There will be many in our lives. Expect it—it is not the problem that is the problem. It is what we do about it. Be a problem solver, not a complainer. Cultivate your faith. Nurture your faith! Expect good things. Look for good things. Do not feed into negativity. Get away from negativity, pessimism, and cynicism. They will only contaminate you. You want to be a winner, so expect the best.

One of the primary characteristics of winners is that they expect to win! Yes, they <u>expect</u> to win. They forge ahead, they keep faith, and they get results!

Your life will follow your expectations. What you expect is what you will get. One of the key elements to enlarging your vision is raising your level of expectancy. In order to change your life, change your thinking.

Start your day with faith and positive expectancy, then go out and expect good things. Try to awaken with confidence and positive anticipation for the day. Expect doors of opportunity to open for you. Expect to excel in your career. Expect to rise above life's challenges.

How many times have you witnessed someone accomplishing a deed simply because they thought they could? A positive mindset going into anything gets the best results. I have witnessed this countless times on the golf course. I have watched talented golfers miss shots because they could not visualize it. They simply lacked confidence in the given shot. On the other hand, I have seen much less skilled golfers hit phenomenal shots because they expected to. They just looked at the target and confidently hit it there. Of course, this kind of confidence comes from practice and hard work in any endeavor. With the work we acquire that positive mindset. We raise our level of self-expectancy, and ultimately of success. We should remember the importance of work. Usually, our confidence is a result of working at something. Practice and work enhance our ability and confidence, which leads to a positive expectation.

If we don't make a habit of expecting good things to come our way, then we are not likely to get anything good. Our expectations set the boundaries for our life. We must look through our "eyes of faith" and start seeing ourselves as happy, healthy, and whole. That means even when your situation looks bleak, when you are despairing or becoming depressed, you must encourage yourself. The more we believe in ourselves and respect ourselves, the more others will believe in and respect us. Be your own best friend. Sometimes in life we have to be our own best cheerleader!

Chapter 10

On Obstacles/Struggles

*"Serenity is not freedom from the storm,
but peace amidst the storm."*

*"I shall smile, for my smile conveys my
faith that God is always in charge. We
shall not be discouraged or puzzled with
our problems. That is our practice. It is the
practice which God appoints us, and is
having its work in making us patient, and
humble, and generous, and unselfish, and
kind, and courteous.*

We shall not grudge the hand that is molding the still shapeless image within us. We are growing more beautiful; though we see it not, and our tribulation is adding to our perfection. Therefore, keep in the midst of life. Do not isolate yourself. Be among men, and among things, and among troubles, and difficulties, and obstacles. Talent develops itself in solitude. Character is the mainstream of life."
—Goethe

"Should you shield the canyons from the windstorms, you would never see the true beauty of their carvings."
—Elisabeth Kübler-Ross

It is in tough times that we find out what we are really made of. God does not always change circumstances as much as He changes us with trials. We often expect circumstances to change, but it works the other way. If we can change our attitudes, God will change the circumstances. Don't give up, don't quit, don't whine, and complain, wondering why something is happening. Stand strong and fight the good fight of faith.

Adversity is a constant in the world—we all experience it. It is in the depths of adversity that we solve much. We are challenged for a resolution, which explains the adage, "necessity is the mother of invention."

Walk through your adversities with your head up, your grit and determination strong, and be patient. The strong survive because they find ways to rise above their adversities. You may be tested—you may bend a little from those inevitable headwinds. Remember, one foot ahead, steady, methodical, always hopeful, and embracing patience.

My father used to say, "It is a great life if it doesn't weaken." He was a young man trying to get along in the midst of the Great Depression–era 1930s. He saw people struggling everywhere to make it, including himself. I suspect that saying came out of the 1930s.

America was faced with challenges in a decade that tried people's souls. It was one of the most difficult periods in the history of our country. People endured and persevered through the hardships of drought, famine, unemployment, very little income, and all sorts of things brought by the Depression. It challenged people to the limits of their patience, endurance, and exhaustion. It did pass eventually, as things do, and a new era of prosperity came.

We have heard it said, "adversities and problems build character." Obviously, this is hard to believe, much less accept, when we are toughly challenged. We do not grow as much when everything goes our way as when we are tested. Rather than complain, why not rejoice in the new day? We are taught to enjoy the season, whether it brings plenty or struggle. Again, train your mind to see the good, and to be grateful for what you have. Every season is not springtime. There has to be planting seasons, watering seasons, and maintaining seasons, when you're pulling weeds and tilling the soil. Without going through the process, you are not going to come into a new season of harvest. Remember, work and patience come before the payoff. Instead of being frustrated by the difficulties, have a new perspective. <u>The season you are in is preparing you for your future success.</u>

God has given you the grace you need to not only endure this season, but to also enjoy the season. When you are content, you see each day as a gift. You appreciate the people in your life. You are getting stronger and developing your character. You will come out of fall and winter, and come into your springtime. Things will begin to bloom and blossom once again. Don't go through life wanting something else. SEE the gift in what you have right now. "These are the good old days."

"If plants are certain of a coming spring, through which they will come out of themselves, why cannot I a human plant, be certain of a spring to come, in which I will be able to fulfill myself?"
—Kahlil Gibran

"If rivers come out of their icy prison thus bright and immortal, shall not I too resume my spring life with joy and hope? Have I no hopes to sparkle on the surface of life's current?"
—Henry David Thoreau

I would like to share a brief story about a golf buddy of mine. He has had 13 different surgeries over the years. Many of his surgeries have been very challenging to work through and still be able to play decent golf, such as four knee replacements, a neck fusion, two shoulder surgeries on each shoulder, and a number of hernia surgeries. He is now 67 years old and, of course, still plays golf. There is no question he has some impairments related to all those surgeries. I have never heard him complain or use that as an alibi. He simply moves along and does the best he can. He even shares a few jokes and banters with the rest of us. He personifies perseverance and a great attitude, and makes no excuses. I do not think he even realizes what a terrific role model he is. Often, our challenge in life is to deal with obstacles and struggles, and to participate as wounded warriors, simply doing the best we can.

As this goes to print, my friend just had open heart surgery, we all know he will be back swinging a golf club soon, it is who he is; a relentless fighter.

Chapter 11

On Honesty/Integrity

*"The path to self-respect and others respect
is honesty and integrity."*

Benjamin Franklin is credited with saying "Honesty is the best policy." Being honest in a relationship is very important because no relationship can be successful without trust. Being completely honest in life can be difficult, but is the only proper path. Being truthful has many rewards. Honesty gives us the power to handle tough circumstances in life as people around us will trust us. Honesty also means to honor and respect the feelings of others.

Honesty is a reflection of your own thoughts and feelings. If you want people to know who you really are, be honest in your self-reflection.

Courage is not absence of fear. It takes courage to say what you feel. Being honest with yourself and with others shows how much you really care. It demonstrates self-respect and respect for others.

Honesty encourages affection and love and sets an example that invites others to imitate. This kind of authenticity creates loving relationships. A mature person conveys honest expression in a style that minimizes painful impact. Honesty can bring people closer by creating a safe connection, and both parties feel secure enough to be genuine in their interactions. Being authentic is to say what you feel. It breaks us free of the limitations of fear. With honesty you will become very attractive to other honest people, which is very enriching. Keep a clean slate by staying honest. Honesty keeps us out of trouble.

Dishonesty often stems from self-centeredness. We may cover up or hide things for our own gain. If we are to walk with confidence, we must possess integrity! Do the right thing. If we want self-respect and others' respect, integrity is imperative.

Down through the ages, many things were settled by a handshake. A person's word was their word. Let's be dependable! Part of honesty is being accountable to what we say we are doing or going to do.

Being honest shows a good and clean character that stimulates the same behavior. Honesty leads towards a clear conscience and peaceful mind. Honesty and integrity are respected by friends, family, and society, which leads to happiness. It is one of the virtues that is said to be esteemed more than silver and gold.

Integrity covers a lot of ground. When we hear of a person of "good integrity," we want to be their friend. It is expected that person will be very forthright and trustworthy. They do not have an ulterior motive. They are transparent and we count on them doing the right thing. They tend to look at the whole picture, not simply what is right for them—rather, what is best for the masses. They are responsible, credible, and of good character. To be called a person of integrity is one the highest compliments we could receive.

Honesty can help health and wellness. If we want to be the best we can be, it starts with honesty. If we are trying to be someone we are not, we will not flourish. Honesty leads to self-compassion—it allows us to set realistic goals. It increases our courage and frees us to be our best self.

I read a great story of Abe Lincoln displaying true honesty. In managing and old country store, as in everything he did for others, Lincoln did his very best. He was honest and cordial and always patient and extending to his customers.

Late one evening, while counting over his cash, he realized he had shorted one customer a few cents the he owed. Upon closing the store, he walked quite a distance to make it right.

Another time he discovered one morning that a scale he had used the previous night was inaccurate. The lady he weighed tea for did not get her appropriate amount. So Lincoln determined the correct amount and took it to the lady, who of course, did not know she had been shorted.

And so it was that Abraham Lincoln became known as "Honest Abe." This quality certainly bode well for his political journey.

Chapter 12

On Meaning/Spirituality

"Let us journey in the right direction,
with sound values and clear vision."

One of my favorite adages is, "The greatest use of life is to spend it on something that will out-live it." We all have a vain sense of immortality. We'd like to be remembered. Some have written songs, books, created painting, etc. Not all of us will make a profound impact on society or attain greatness.

However, the intent is noble. We'd like to achieve and aspire to our best potential. But a wise man knows, "All of our successes are but a fleeting thing." Man's greatness is transitory.

Let's give our attention to things that last: faith, hope, love, charity, etc., with a vision of a further, more substantial home. Working and striving for a secular goal is mostly shallow vanity. We would like to be about more than simply material possessions.

In recent years we hear about success versus significance. For many years self-help books empathized how to be successful. How to be a winner. Often success was measured by material wealth. Then Rick Warren came out with a book titled, *The Purpose Driven Life*. As best I could determine, the thesis was, life should be evaluated on its significance and meaning, not simply on success as the world typically thinks of it. At the end of the day, what meaning/significance did we get?

You see, life is more about a journey than a destination. Let us journey in the right direction, with sound values and clear vision!

It would seem the goals of religion down through the ages was to give society a code of morality to live by as well as a belief in a future life. Both religion and spirituality teach there is more to the universe than meets the eye, and more to our life than the physical body. Both agree that there are non-physical elements to the universe, and to our existence, and that unless we consciously connect with them, we will never be truly fulfilled in life. Religion presents a set of beliefs, dogmas, and "holy men" as an intermediary between you and spirit—spirituality promotes your own individual explanation in defining and connecting to spirit as it fits your heart and mind.

Religion and spirituality can come together. Many people find spirituality within their religion. Religion promotes shame and guilt. Spirituality promotes self-honesty and awareness. It has been said that religion asks you to sacrifice your present attachments for a promised future. Spirituality asks you to let go of your present attachments for a better present.

Spirituality can fill the gaps left by both organized religion and by science. Religion says the truth is what the scriptures say, and you must believe it. Science says that truth is only the facts that can be proven. Spirituality says that reason is not the only means of knowing, but that this doesn't mean one needs to have blind faith in religious doctrines either. We accept how little we know about the universe and about ourselves and explore a deeper meaning in life through tools such as meditation, contemplation, and self-exploration—and also reason, scriptures, or anything we may get ahold of.

The primary difference between religion and spirituality is that spirituality can debate with science, while religion can't. The whole meditation and mindfulness movement in recent decades is a result of this debate: science investigating spiritual practices.

"Science brings knowledge; spirituality brings meaning.
Both are important."
—Giovanni

Chapter 13

On Gratitude

*"Cultivate the healing forces in gratitude,
affirm the good things in life."*

Be thankful. Harness the healing forces in gratitude. Appreciation for what we have can lift depression that comes from dwelling on what we don't have. The mind can only hold one idea at a time. Cancel out the gloom of a minus by making yourself focus on a satisfying plus. Reverse your affirmations. Sometimes that can be as easy as, rather than dwelling on a problem, focus on a solution. Thoughts in our mind dominate and determine the realities in our lives.

Emerson said, "A man is what he thinks about all day long." The goal is to shake up the internal, dysfunctional negative thoughts with positive functional ones.

Robert Emmons is considered the world's leading expert on gratitude. Gratitude has two key components: first, it is an affirmation of goodness. Second, it is that we recognize the source of this goodness is outside ourselves.

Also remember:
1. Gratitude allows celebration of the present.
2. It blocks toxic emotions, (envy, resentment, regret, depression).
3. Grateful people are more stress resilient.
4. It strengthens social ties and self-worth.

"Affirm the good things in life. Gratitude unlocks the fullness of life, making things right, turns what we have into enough, and more. It turns denial into acceptance, chaos to order, confusion to clarity. It can turn a meal into a feast, a house into a home, a stranger into a friend. Gratitude makes sense of our past, brings peace for today, and creates a vision for tomorrow. There is no situation or circumstance so small or large that is not susceptible to gratitude's power."
—Melody Beattie

Even as it may be hard to avoid self-pity entirely, mentally strong people choose to exchange self-pity for gratitude. Giving thanks can transform our lives. Gratitude opens the door to more relationships. Showing appreciation not only helps win more friends, it is the only reasonable disposition.

Gratitude improves physical health. Grateful people experience less aches and pains and report feeling healthier than other people. Grateful people are also more likely to take care of themselves, getting exercise and eating healthy. Gratitude improves psychological health. It literally reduces many negative emotions, like anger, resentment, and self-pity. It has been studied and confirmed that gratitude increases happiness and reduces depression.

Gratitude enhances empathy and reduces aggression. Grateful people can be patient and kind, even when others are less friendly. They experience more sensitivity and empathy toward other people and a decreased desire to seek revenge.

Grateful people sleep better. Simply writing down a few grateful feelings before bed can enhance your sleep. Grateful people are able to appreciate other people's accomplishments. Gratitude reduces social comparisons, which allows our self-esteem to flourish. We then are not resentful about the success of others.

Gratitude increases mental health. Gratitude not only reduces stress, but appears to be valuable in overcoming trauma. Recognizing all you have to be thankful for—even during traumatic times—enhances resilience.

Methods to enhance gratitude can be as simple as keeping a gratitude journal. Just listing five things for which we are grateful each week is a way. Another could be upon waking each morning and recognizing our blessings, trying to be mindful. Challenges in our life can often make it more difficult to embrace gratitude. Our challenge to benefit from gratitude is, rather than occasionally feeling more grateful, to actually be a more grateful person. By consciously counting our blessings and developing more grateful thinking, we actually eliminate ungrateful thoughts. This process helps guard against taking things for granted, and allows us to see the gifts in our life. When we truly become our brother's keeper, we have gratitude for what we can give as opposed to what we receive.

A Christian Confederate Soldier's Prayer

(Anon - alleged to have been found on a CSA casualty
at the Devil's Den, Gettysburg)

I asked God for strength, that I might achieve.
I was made weak, that I might learn humbly to obey.
I asked for health, that I might do greater things.
I was given infirmity, that I might do better things.
I asked for riches, that I might be happy.
I was given poverty, that I might be wise.
I asked for power that I might have the praise of men.
I was given weakness, that I might feel the need of God.
I asked for all things, that I might enjoy life.
I was given life, that I might enjoy all things.
I got nothing that I asked for but
got everything I had hoped for.
Almost despite myself, my unspoken prayers were answered.
I am, among all people, most richly blessed.

Chapter 14

On Compassion

"A compassionate person is kind to every living thing."

Every major religion gives compassion a high place as a virtue in human nature. The Dalai Lama said, "compassion is a necessity, not a luxury, and that without it humanity cannot survive." This moves it from a divine attribute to a practical human necessity for the survival of mankind.

Compassion is an emotion similar to love—however, it is uniquely related to suffering. Compassion is the feeling of empathy we have towards the suffering of others, and the desire to help. Compassion can be deep and passionate and motivate vigorous action. The root word of compassion is "co-suffering"—hence it shares the suffering, and motivates action to help. Compassion is desirable as a key motivator of people. In particular, it motivates them to not only feel the pain of those suffering, but also enhances their desire to <u>alleviate it.</u> It identifies with others in an empathetic way. It is the opposite reaction to people that cause suffering. Those people are ruthless and cruel. The compassionate person will respond to the humanity of others, not their ethnicity or religion.

Compassion is a great blessing from God upon mankind. A compassionate person is kind to every living being on Earth. He is not cruel to anyone. An old Sioux Indian expression essentially said, "<u>We are all one with Mother Earth.</u>" If we have compassion for others, only then do others have compassion for us. A cruel person is dealt with cruelly by others. A compassionate person is loved by everyone. When he is in need, others will help in whatever way they can. Therefore, people who are helped in their need must help others in need.

A compassionate person will seek to help the suffering. It is the opposite of the attitude that causes war and many evils. An individual who cannot empathize with the suffering of another human beings will not only ignore the suffering of others, but may even contribute to the suffering. No one can feel the exact pain. Empathy, however, will enter into that unique experience and connect one individual to another, allowing them to perceive another's pain and suffering. Suffering can be psychological, physical, and social. Physical suffering is usually easy to see and recognize. The psychological and social dysfunction of suffering is not so easily seen. Compassion helps identify it, and give motivation to relieve the suffering of others.

I recently heard an excellent Mother Teresa story of compassion. A gentleman traveled to Calcutta, India to meet her. Upon arriving, he contacted her to arrange a meeting. She agreed and asked the gentleman to pick her up at 4:00 a.m. the next morning. So they meet and started driving though Calcutta. Upon seeing a man lying on the sidewalk Mother Teresa asked to pull over. She got out and went up to this guy and comforted him till help arrived—she told him he was saved.

They continued driving along and saw another man lying close to the road. They pulled over and Mother Teresa instructed the driver to go help him. The driver got out and went over to this man. The stench almost turned him away. But he knelt down and offered help. He told the man he was saved. Getting back in the car, the driver told Mother Teresa, "thank you for showing me compassion," upon which she said, "Do not thank me. Thank the man on the street."

We should be thankful for having people to serve.

Chapter 15

On Empathy

" Can we walk in another's moccasins?"

We are all who we are because of where we've been. In other words, to some extent, we are the sum total of our experiences. Between our orientation, environment, and experiences, coupled with our genetic makeup, we are a personality.

This realization should give us an understanding about people. Let's not be too quick to judge others. We don't know their story, the burdens, and the obstacles they may have.

It has been said, "To be tender with the young, compassionate with the aged, sympathetic with the striving, and tolerant of the weak and wrong!" Sometimes in life, you will have been all of these. Accept people the way they are and the way they are not!

It costs us nothing to smile at others and encourages them to smile back. Perhaps they forget their burdens for a minute, and we lighten their day. Our BELIEF and FAITH in others RAISES them up to a higher level. We can positively influence others by how we attend to them. It is our God-given duty to be a friend.

Most leaders such as teachers or coaches understand how to motivate. They raise the individual's confidence by encouragement and having positive expectations for them. They help us believe in ourselves by believing in us. Whenever you catch someone doing something right, tell them how good or special they are. This will reinforce positive behavior and make you both feel better. Look to lift others up.

Empathy involves the ability to emotionally feel what the other person is experiencing. Essentially, it is putting yourself in someone else's position and feeling what they must be feeling. Empathy leads to helping behavior, which benefits social relationships. We are naturally social creatures. Things that aid in our relationships with other people benefit us as well. When people experience empathy, they are more likely to engage in prosocial behaviors that benefit other people. Not only are you more likely to engage in helpful behaviors when you feel empathy for other people, but other people are also more likely to help you when they experience empathy. By understanding what people are thinking and feeling, people are able to respond appropriately in social situations.

While empathy might fail sometimes, most people are able to empathize with others in a variety of situations. This ability to see things from another person's perspective and sympathize with another's emotions plays an important role in our social lives. Empathy allows us to understand others and quite often compels us to take action to relieve another person's suffering.

Listening is one of the most important ways we can show empathy. Be fully attentive, not distracted with anything else. To fully listen, be fully present, and look the person in the eye. Often empathy can be shown by sharing our own vulnerabilities—opening up about ourselves can help convey to the other person that they are not alone. If you know the person and are comfortable, displays of affection help to create a bond, such as a hug. A kiss on each cheek is common in some Middle East cultures. I once had a friend from that culture, who, upon meeting a Swedish girl, gave her a hug and kiss on the cheek. Of course, she was shocked, as she was unaccustomed to such a greeting. But he simply winked at me and told her it was a traditional greeting. Had we not been college kids, and she not accepted his humor, he could have been slapped.

Chapter 16

On Friendship

"Treat others as you would be treated."

As Thoreau said, "The most I can do for my friend is simply to be his friend."

It is usually not our place to tell our friends how to live, or as the saying goes, "Be leery of giving advice. Fools won't heed it, and wise men don't need it." Other people's problems make poor bedfellows. They are usually better equipped to deal with them than us. But be there for support when needed.

Cultivate your friendships! Remember the scripture, "Love thy neighbor as thyself." It truly is in giving and serving that we can find meaning and fulfillment.

We seek our friends in times of joy as well as sorrow. The communion of two souls is a comfort on the journey.

The things most worthwhile to give do not diminish with our having given them, i.e., a smile, a word of encouragement, a pat on the back! Think about that—the things most worth giving are not material, they are simply common consideration and kindness. Our reward back is a content soul and an inner glow.

"One who has unreliable friends soon comes to ruin, but there is a friend who sticks closer than a brother."
—Proverbs 18:24

We all know how warm and inviting it is when we meet someone and they extend their hand with a smile, and say how nice it is to meet you. If we would like friends, remember the golden rule, "Treat others as you would be treated." Hospitality, kindness, and compassion will bring friends.

When given the opportunity, make a compliment. Compliments help people rise up, do more, and go further than they ever thought they could because someone believed in them.

We hold a lot of the potential in another by how we attend to that person. Be a bolster to others, not an obstacle! The way we see others is the way we treat them, and the way we treat them is the way they often become. We have the potential to stimulate and mold them to their best potential.

A friend is kind and considerate, and looks beyond themselves. Humility and kindness are some of the noblest traits of being a friend.

Friendship is about knowing someone better than others do and counting on them whenever the need arises. A friend is like a gift that one gives himself. It is very difficult to experience the fullness of life without friends. Honesty, trust, and authenticity are some of the qualities that allow us to remain true to a friend, and allow them a shoulder to lean on all the time. Friendships form a bond that enhances a meaningful life.

A good friend is available irrespective of circumstances. A true friend accepts you unconditionally, tolerates your shortcomings, and encourages you even in the face of hopelessness. With a loyal friend you can be yourself without judgment because you know they understand you.

A good friend brings out the best in someone by encouraging and pushing them to make the best out of their abilities and strengths. We have all heard it said, "a friend in need, is a friend indeed." Pick your friends closely and cultivate them; they influence your life!

Friendship brings people together to form a greater and stronger whole than its individual parts. They seek to soar beyond limits as a single determined force.

Lying on our death beds, it is not likely we will be thinking of how hard we worked and how much money we have. True happiness is not based on material possessions, your power, or your status! Rather, it is based on the quality of your relationships with the people you love and respect. Having a network of close relationships to sustain and nurture us along our path and challenges is so very important. Surround yourself with people who will enhance your growth and help you be more of who you are.

Chapter 17

On Giving

"Anything of value in life only multiplies when it is given."

The more we give, the more we receive because we will keep the law of abundance of the universe circulating in our life. In fact, anything that is of value in life only multiplies when it is given. When we extend hospitality and service to others, we are stimulated to do more. The return is directly proportional to the giving when it is unconditional and from the heart. That is why the act of giving has to be joyful.

Practicing the Law of Giving is actually very simple: if you want joy, give joy to others; if you want love, learn to give love; if you want attention and appreciation, learn to give attention and appreciation; if you want material affluence, help other become materially affluent. The easiest way to get what you want is to help others get what they want. If you want to be blessed with all the good things in life, learn to silently bless everyone with all the good things in life.

The best way of putting the Law of Giving into operation is to decide that anytime you come in contact with anyone you will give them something. It does not have to be material—it can be a flower, a compliment, or a prayer. In fact, the most powerful forms of giving are non-material. The gifts of caring, attention, affection, appreciation and love are some of the most precious gifts you can give, and they don't cost you anything. Make a decision to give wherever you go, to whomever you see. As long as you are giving, you will be receiving. The more you give, the more confidence you will gain in the miraculous effects of the Law.

Our true nature is one of affluence and abundance. We are naturally affluent because nature supports every need. The source of all wealth is the conscientiousness that knows how to fulfill every need, including joy, love, laughter, peace, harmony and knowledge. If you seek these things first for yourself and others, all else will come to you spontaneously.

It is easy to be on the wrong scent in the pursuit of happiness. Is it all about our getting stuff and our satisfactions, or could it be also about giving?

It is the man who is the missionary, it is not his words.

The universal language is love, a smile, and compassion. In the heart of Africa, black men and women can remember the only white man they ever saw: David Livingston. Deep within that Dark Continent, people's faces lit up, as they talked about the kind doctor who passed there years before. They could not understand him—but they felt the love within him.

Albert Schweitzer was known to have said, "As for you, I know not what your destiny may be, but one thing I do know, the only ones among you will be truly happy, are those who have sought and found how to serve."

The test of religion is not religiousness, but Love. Not what we have done, not what we have believed, not what we have achieved, but how we have discharged the common charities of life. We have our wrong doings, (sins), but we shall also be judged by what we have not done, by sins of omission. What could we have done? What can we do?

Success needs to be about much more than material things—they come and go. We all need money, but don't allow it to be the primary focus. Focusing on a dream, a cause, or having a mission, is what lends meaning. Success is the result of service, and money usually follows. So find what you love, give to others, and happiness will follow.

The things most worthy to give do not diminish with our having given them.

Chapter 18

On Forgiveness

"To be at peace with ourselves and others,
we need forgiveness."

Forgiveness is one of those things you cannot see or touch but it is real. Forgiveness is so powerful that it changes a person's heart. It is important to forgive others their wrongs so that we can be at peace and move on with our lives. It is also important to forgive yourself of the things you have done wrong and the times that you have caused others pain. This will help you be at peace with yourself. Also when you forgive others it improves your health. Unforgiveness may cause many of the psychosomatic illnesses we experience. This phenomenon is well-documented.

The Lord says to forgive others as He has forgiven you. We have all made mistakes. We have all hurt others. Think of the mistakes you have made. Think of the times you have hurt others either intentionally or by accident. Do you want forgiveness? Do you need forgiveness? The Lord forgives us. It is the way He shows His love for us. He wants us to do the same. Forgiveness is not always easy but to be at peace with others and with God, it is necessary. It may take time to forgive, but it will be worth it. It may be a process, it may not happen all at once, but when it does you will ultimately be glad you quit carrying that load.

Forgiving someone is a choice we make. You make a choice by your will to forgive and let go. It is a deliberate, or purposeful act. It does not mean the other person is not wrong. It just means you forgive them. You let the anguish go.

Sometimes the hardest person to forgive is ourselves. Maybe you have hurt someone by things you have said, or done. The guilt can be eating you alive. You may feel you don't deserve to be forgiven. Do what you can to make amends. Ask the person to forgive you. And whether they do or not, you must forgive yourself. You must do this for yourself and the people around you. It is hard to live in harmony with others if you are feeling guilty or sad. You may not even know how it is affecting others or yourself. But it is. Forgive yourself. Let it go. It does not remove hurt, but it allows us to move on.

"If one cannot forgive, bring two shovels."
—Attributed to Confucius

A lady bought a parrot for a pet. All the parrot did was treat her badly. It insulted her and every time she tried to pick it up, it would peck at her arm.

One day she had enough of the parrot and as it was insulting her, she picked it up, and it continued with its insults. "You're ugly! I can't stand you!" and pecked at her arm as she carried it. She opened the freezer door and threw him in and closed the door. From inside, the parrot was still going on for about five seconds and then suddenly went quiet.

She thought, "Oh no, I killed it." She opened the door and the parrot just looked at her. She picked it up. Then the parrot said, "I am very sorry. I apologize for my bad behavior and I promise you there will be no more of that. From now on, I will be a respectful, obedient parrot."

"Well OK." she said. "Apology accepted."

The parrot said, "Thank you." Then he said, "Can I ask you something?"

"Yes, what?" she said.

And the parrot looked at the freezer and asked, "What did the chicken do?"

Chapter 19

On Humility

*"God will lift up those who humble themselves down
and give service to others."*

Humility is a word that is often heard but not fully understood by many. It can be thought of as putting oneself down or feeling worthless. Humility is not defined that way. Humility is more than not calling attention to yourself or thinking someone is better. Humility is a value that is manifested through acceptance, selflessness and contentment.

An example of acceptance in humility could simply be accepting advice from other people regarding changes for the better. No one can deny the fact that everyone makes mistakes and nobody is perfect. Everyone needs improvement. If other people give advice, it is always better to take that and evaluate whether it can help. It is one way of opening ourselves and pondering new ideas and values that come from other people's opinion and advice. Many people are afraid to accept change because of pride. These things give identity to a person and they fear losing a title, a recognition, and things they are proud of. If there is an acceptance of changes based on other people's advice, then humility is present. The mindset of a humble person is there are things others know that I do not know. People can learn more things if pride, the opposite of humility, is lowered.

Humility is a value that is expressed through selflessness. Performing service and charity anonymously shows humility, performing service to others even if they don't see it, is a clear form of selflessness. What others think does not matter, we are doing acts without applause and recognition. It is good to think of others more that yourself. God will lift up those who humble themselves down and give service to others. Additionally, the feeling is always good when one gives service to others.

Humility is also expressed through contentment. We need not demand more blessings. This life contains many worldly possessions. It is common for people to always want more in their lives. This leads to a sense of competition, wanting the best. And then perhaps being boastful. People should be content with what they have at the moment. Some people may look to a higher power and appreciate with a sense of humility—they are blessed.

> *"Humility is greatness*
> *in plain clothes.*
> *Humility is royalty*
> *without a crown."*
> —Spencer Kimball

Chapter 20

On Perception

"We do not see the world as it is, but rather as we are."

> *"I see worlds of*
> *ugliness about*
> *me; there must be*
> *worlds of ugliness*
> *within me."*
> —Kahlil Gibran

Our perception of things is usually a mirrored reflection (projection) of our own inner feelings. We can see a speck in our brother's eye, not realizing we have a log in our own.

If we are uncomfortable with our own experience, situation, or circumstance, let's not blame others. Let's look to ourselves for an explanation. We get out of life what we put into it. Perhaps we need to adjust ourselves, since the world will not adjust to us.

We do not see the world as it is, but rather as we are. Perception is our sensory experience of the world around us. This involves recognizing environmental stimuli and the actions that are responses to those stimuli. Perception is key to gaining information and an understanding of the world around us. Without it, we would not be able to survive in this world filled with stimuli flying all around us. This is because perception not only molds our experience of the world but allows us to act within our environment.

If we are well adjusted and have a sense of balance in our lives, our perception will typically be somewhat accurate. However, if we are a bit angry, bitter, hateful, or full of some type of negativity, our opinion and experience may well be clouded and distorted. The bottom line is we have perceptions of people and things. We cannot always trust our perceptions. Sometimes we need to discuss our "take on things" with close friends. We need to get away from our bias, get out of judgment mode, and see things as they are—not as they seem through our distorted image.

A little story on distorted perception. I have been going to a gym for a number of years. I do a fair amount of weight training. So one time while at a swimming pool, my brother asked how my workouts were going. So of course, being the cocky brother, I simply flexed my muscles and said, "Do you think I look like this by accident?" Of course, a well-buffed mean machine. Upon which my brother laughed and said, "You obviously have a distorted mirror. Everyone should have a mirror like that." Obviously implying I was delusional, and saw myself better than reality.

We all know mirrors don't lie. I had been working hard for years and had an accurate image of who I was. He was simply a competitive, jealous, younger brother. He was an occasional workout guy, how could he possibly be in my condition?

Pay the Price

Chapter 21

On Mindfulness

"Mindfulness puts us into the present moment rather than rehashing the past or imagined future."

Mindfulness has almost become cliché in recent years! I have always told my children to "be about what they are about." When I am talking to you, get off your phone. Make eye contact and be attentive. When you greet someone, don't give a half-greeting. Look at those people and be personable. Have the discipline to digest and respond to the moment. If you experience something special, be in the moment—see it, feel it, contemplate it. The only thing real right now is what is in front of you. The present time. If we are thinking of past or future events, we miss the present. The present is all we have now. This reminds me of the process of decision making. One classic example of mindfulness can be explained by decision making. Procrastination robs us of being attentive to the moment.

We all will be faced with making many decisions in our life. Some are life altering and require more deliberation than others. The moment of absolute certainty may never come. After a reasonable amount of thought and deliberation, pull the trigger. Make your best decision and move on. Excessive procrastination simply robs us of current pleasures and experiences.

Mindfulness means maintaining a moment-by-moment awareness of our thoughts, feelings, bodily sensations, and surrounding environment through a gentle nurturing lens. Mindfulness also involves acceptance, meaning we pay attention to our thoughts and feelings without judging them, without necessarily believing there is a right and wrong way to think or feel in a given moment. When we practice mindfulness, our thoughts tune in to what we're sensing in the present moment, rather than rehashing the past or imagining the future.

Many forms of fear, such as worry and anxiety, are caused by too much concern about the future, and not enough presence. Many forms of non-forgiveness, such as guilt, anger, resentment, and bitterness are caused by too much concern about the past, and not enough presence. A true state of consciousness frees us from past and future. It brings a sense of liberation and salvation.

The principle of mindfulness is to stay centered in the Now! Give your fullest attention to whatever the moment presents. Try to give more attention to the Doing than the Result you want to achieve. This also means that you completely accept what is, because you cannot give your full attention to something and at the same time resist it.

As soon as you honor the present moment, all unhappiness and struggle dissolve, and life begins to flow with joy and ease. When you act out of present-moment awareness, whatever you do becomes imbued with a sense of quality, care, and love. So, do not be concerned with the fruit of your action—give attention to the action itself. The fruit will come as it will. Krishna told Arjuna, we have the right to our actions, but not the fruit of our actions. The fruit is out of our hands and resides with Fate: God's simplest action, or a Higher Power. Concentrate on doing a good job and be unattached to outcomes. Peace lives here.

Live Each Day to the Fullest

Get the most from each hour, each day, and each age of your life

Then you can look forward with confidence and back without regret

Be yourself, but be your best self,

Dare to be different and to follow your own star

And don't be afraid to be happy

Enjoy what is beautiful

Love with all of your heart and soul

Believe that those you love, love you

Forget what you have done for your friends

and remember what they have done for you

Disregard what the world owes you and

concentrate on what you owe the world

When you are faced with a decision, make the decision

as wisely as possible–then forget it

The moment of absolute certainty never arrives

Blessed is the generation in which the old listen to the young

And double-blessed is the generation in which the young listen to the old.

—The Talmud

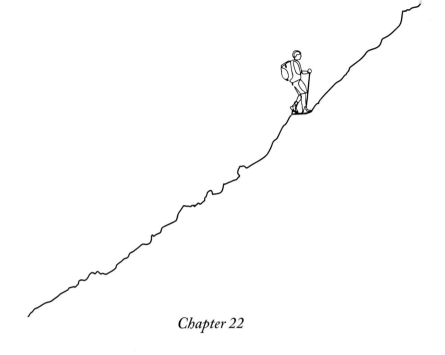

Chapter 22

On Finances

"Moderation in spending allows freedom."

*"I didn't believe you when
you said you didn't need
anyone, but now I see
that living in this world
without wanting anything
has always been the true
teaching; and that not
pushing the river is living in
the will of God."*
—Author Unknown

This is quite simple and basic. Spend less than you make, invest the difference, allowing interest to compound. This investment can take many and varied forms, e.g., stocks, bonds, real estate, etc. Never—I repeat, *never*—put all your eggs in one basket. Diversify, which has withstood the test of time for most people in most situations. There is usually a variance of return on investment between different investment vehicles—and some can drop in value fast. Diversifying helps keep a good average.

Typically, the higher return on an investment, the higher the risk. Do not be naïve to this fact. If we are going to have a consistent savings plan, which grows with interest, be sure it is balanced and not over weighted in high-risk vehicles. It is hard to grow savings if you actually lose money, or principal. It would be prudent to always remember what our elders taught us, "If it is too good to be true, it probably is." Do not be over zealous or greedy. Wealth is typically accrued slow and steady.

Strive as hard as you can to build a "rainy day fund." This should be an amount one can live on for close to six months. This is highly recommended by financial advisors. This is an emergency fund in the event of something like a job loss or other unforeseen tragedies. This is money we do not spend on anything else. This lends itself to a comfort and peace of mind. It will serve you well throughout your life.

When I say to invest the difference between what you earn and what you spend—I suggest this amount be no less than 10% of your earnings. Most folks live on credit and installment plans. Avoid this like the plague! It merely allows one to live beyond their means and encourages a relentless cycle of debt. Modern America is extremely consumptive and materialistic.

Our older generation remembers a time of no television. There was only radio. In the middle to later 1950's televisions came out. They were in living rooms throughout America. Some years later credit cards became accessible. Now, we were bombarded with advertisements right into our homes, and eventually they were even in living color. Many of the purchases offered installment payments. Now, couple all of that with credit card availability in the hands of hungry, consumptive, undisciplined people. This lead to an indebtedness that the typical American had never experienced. It was easy to purchase almost anything impulsively. We only needed that credit card or installment plan. The lesson learned by many was to only purchase what they could afford.

So keep your material desires simple, always remembering two things about possessions:

1. Possessions in themselves, particularly the more extravagant ones that aren't necessary for reasonable living, do not make you happy.
2. Indulgent possessions come with a price. We become tools of our tools. Lest we sell our souls for possessions, we should keep our material desires humble.

One of the basic premises of Buddhism is that life is suffering. Suffering is caused by craving and aversion. Rather than constantly struggling to get what you want, try to modify your wanting. Wanting deprives us of contentment and happiness. True happiness and contentment can be attained by giving up useless cravings and learn to live each day one at a time. Not dwelling in the past or imagined future, we become happy and free. Look closer in the Mindfulness chapter.

"He is a wise man who does not grieve for the things which he has not, but rejoices for those which he has."
—Epictetus

Many have heard it said, "The love of money is the root of all evil." It does not say money is evil. We are allowed to prosper and enjoy our lives, and have material success. However, we are not to worship it. It can enhance our lives, yet stand guard it does not own or corrupt our lives. It is our responsibility to share some of our abundance somewhere! Our lives are not simply about us. When money becomes a driving force and has unbalanced importance, we will never find peace.

I could go on and on about financial responsibility. I would like to simply repeat "spend less than you earn." The most basic habit to cultivate is money management!

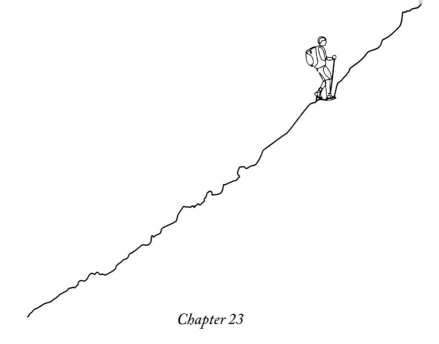

Chapter 23

On Physical Fitness/Health

*"For those who
don't make time for
exercise, they'll have
to make time for
illness."*
—Edward Stanley

To perform at our best level, we need to pay attention to our physical health. What do we put into our bodies? How much sleep do we get? What state of physical health do we have? Most peak performers pay attention to these three things.

Exercise is a great stress reliever! The goal is to make it a habit, and to be disciplined enough to consistently get exercise. I have found most people who are fit are also more resilient to adversities and challenges. Their strength of body adds to a strength of mind.

Take care of your body—it is your engine, and we only get one.

Sticking to an exercise program contributes to lower blood pressure levels. Constant physical activity helps keep your arteries clear, improves your circulatory system, and maintains good heart health. Another benefit of being physically fit is that you will burn more calories and manage your weight. You will increase muscle mass, lower your body fat, and boost your body's resting metabolic rate. Regular weight-bearing exercise, such as strength training, running, biking, exerts stress on your body's skeletal system. This helps with bone health, which fends off osteoporosis, a concern as we age.

Regular exercise provides various anti-aging benefits. High-intensity workouts stimulate muscle growth and build lean muscle, which reduces aging effects. Exercise also increases brain cell health, which helps with better cognitive functioning.

Strive for a healthy mind in a healthy body. Exercise releases dopamine and serotonin, the neurotransmitters that give your body that "feel good" sensation. As a result, you will be more relaxed and maintain a general feeling of happiness during your daily activities.

Seeing the result of regular exercise can boost your self-confidence. Maybe you have lost weight, increased your stamina and endurance, or added strength. These developments ultimately increase your self-esteem. Keeping fit and healthy will be one of the most important things you do for yourself. Staying active will help you stay strong and ward off the likelihood of chronic disease. Not only will you live longer, but you will also have a better quality of life. Staying in good shape gives you more energy to perform everyday tasks at work and at home. That makes it more likely that you'll have energy in your off time when you look forward to leisure and fun.

There are countless examples of people who are too busy to exercise or who are not concerned with healthy living. Sometimes we think we are invincible, or we will start doing it later, and later doesn't come. But health issues do. All we can say when lying in the hospital with a serious health issue is, "I wished I had been proactive and taken better care of myself." Invariably a small effort to do the right thing is much less painful and costly than the consequences of not doing it!

Please try remembering that to really benefit from exercise, it should be consistent, and methodical. It is not an occasional or "sometimes" thing. Expend the effort, "pay the price" of taking care of your health, and the benefits are endless. Regular exercise allows us to do physically challenging things with less difficulty or injury, and gives us the stamina to complete vigorous activities.

One of the fellows at my gym likes to tell a story of why he thinks he is in such good physical shape. He has always been quite active. He walks approximately three miles a day, about five days a week. In addition he does resistance training and weight lifting three times weekly. Recently, he repeated a story he had told to his three sons. "I am sure I am in the top 10% of my age group for being in shape. I can still lift my lawn mower up into the back of my pickup truck alone." He had said several years ago. And he is now 70 years old and doing the same thing. Recently he said, "Now I bet I am in the top 5% of guys my age cause I can still do the same thing!" The years of consistent conditioning allowed him to stay fit and hoped his example would be a role model for his sons.

Conclusion

1. Learn your vocation, obsess about it, this is a lifelong duty and obligation. School is never out for the pro!

2. Set your goals and crystalize them. Understand there will be hardships and setbacks. Keep your eyes on these goals, knowing, understanding, and appreciating the primary tool to accomplishment is determination and perseverance. Perseverance is one of the single most important qualities on the road to success!

3. If we are going to benefit most from this book, we need to contemplate the material and re-read it periodically. Repetition is an aid to memory. Changes do not come easily or quickly. Do the necessary work to get what you want.

4. Employ discipline and make things a habit. The more productive habits we have, the easier the ascent to our goal. One of the most important keys to success is having the discipline to do what we know we should feel, even if we do not feel like it.

5. It is easy to make excuses, however, if we want top level performance, we must accept responsibility, we must be accountable.

6. Striving to have a positive and constructive attitude always pays dividends. Expect to meet your challenges. Expect to accomplish your goals.

7. Be conservative with your material wants. Debt robs us of peace of mind today and encumbers us tomorrow. Live in a manner that does not encumber, but rather promotes freedom.

8. Understand the healing power of GRATITUDE. Count your blessings/celebrate your life.

9. Smile at people, be kind and encouraging, and give something back. Success is about more than ourselves. We are all in this together as part of a world family. A life lived just to satisfy yourself, never really satisfies anyone.

10. Do not quit if you have a dream, a goal, or an ambition. Get the reward of doing it.

11. The pain of non-fulfillment is greater than the pain of doing the tasks.

12. Self reliance is imperative to accomplishment. If you want something, go after it! Remember, if it is meant to be, it is up to me. Usually no one is coming.

13. Walk into the "Arena of Life" with your head up. Arm yourself with these qualities and virtues that enhance your success. If you have "paid the price" you deserve success!

The title for this book was probably stimulated by Coach Vincent Lombardi as well as my high school coach. The message is quite simple, by our efforts we hope to rise. I have tried to single out what I feel are some of the most important values, virtues, principles by which to live. We certainly may not achieve all of them, but they are ideals to aspire for.

My high school coach from a small town in North Dakota was probably tougher that many NFL coaches. He was a lot like a marine drill sergeant. he did not sugarcoat anything, he mostly kicked our butts. He was also the physical education/gym teacher for the entire high school. The entire male student body got to experience him. One day during a Phy. Ed. Class he had our entire class of about 25 guys running around the block adjacent to the school for the entire 45 minutes. His motive was a disciplinarian thing that persisted for about four weeks. It almost killed some of the students. I was running along about in the middle of the pack, which seemed appropriate for me. I was a skinny little sophomore with skinny little legs. My self perception was that I was about where I should be.

Partway through the exercise the coach hollered to me, " Knut, The little bit of weight you are caring, you should be leading the pack". In the subsequent days, before the next class I contemplated this. I thought, if the coach sees it that way, and of course he was big, intimidating, and omnipotent; maybe there is something to it.

So guess what, the next class out, I ran at the front. I raised my self image, my self perception, and tried to continue that type of behavior the rest of my life.

I could not settle for mediocrity, coach would not allow it. I tried to employ that kind of tenacity and perseverance to whatever I could.

My desire to do a writing like this goes back over two decades.

It started with trying to give my sons a little guidance and perhaps insight to help them along their paths. They became accustomed to my giving them various quotations and adages. As time went to long I kept a journal of these things. I suppose I hoped to give then an essay for life long guidance. Because of the excuses of raising a family and a career, and other things I could come up with, I never got it done. So, with the passage of time and semi-retiring, I no longer had an excuse.

This writing has been a very big challenge to me. There have been times when I question if I have anything to bring to the table. Do I have anything to offer that is different, that may be a contribution. Of course my intent is to show some direction, perhaps lend some inspiration.

In my doubts, I hear the infamous words of Sir Winston Churchill echoing through the canyons of time. "when do you quit? You never ever quit".

I hear General George Patton talking about his destiny. He was relieved of his command in the midst of world war II for an incident he did. After some thought and mustering some determination, he said "It is my destiny to be a soldier, I will not be denied". And so I press on with this "little book" as I call it. We are all called to something, I sincerely hope you find your calling. We are all called for different things. Do not judge others that are called for something different. Whenever possible assist others in their calling/endeavors. Be a good neighbor, we are all part of this world family. In the final chapters of your lives, you shall know your lives stood for something.

I hope this book provokes some thoughts, some ideas, and can be meaningful to some of the reading audience. As I was nearing completion of the book, I started to question whether I should be advocating some of its content, as I came up short and questioned my worthiness. After some time soul searching that inconsistency, I found peace. We all come up short, that is simply a function of being human.

Some of our challenges will come easy, some will be a life challenge. The virtues and qualities of character are ideals. It is the striving by which we will be judged. Live your lives with direction, positivity, and passion. Be patient with your journey, and God bless you.

Here are two of my favorite classic poems that say so much about life.

DESIDERATA

GO PLACIDLY amid the noise and the haste, and remember what peace there may be in silence. As far as possible, without surrender, be on good terms with all persons.

Speak your truth quietly and clearly; and listen to others, even to the dull and the ignorant; they too have their story.

Avoid loud and aggressive persons; they are vexatious to the spirit. If you compare yourself with others, you may become vain or bitter, for always there will be greater and lesser persons than yourself.

Enjoy your achievements as well as your plans. Keep interested in your own career, however humble; it is a real possession in the changing fortunes of time.

Exercise caution in your business affairs, for the world is full of trickery. But let this not blind you to what virtue there is; many persons strive for high ideals, and everywhere life is full of heroism.

Be yourself. Especially do not feign affections. Neither be cynical about love; for in the face of all aridity and disenchantment, it is as perennial as the grass.

Take kindly the counsel of years, gracefully surrendering the things of youth.

Nurture strength of spirit to shield you in sudden misfortune. But do not distress yourself with dark imaginings. Many fears are both of fatigue and loneliness.

Beyond a wholesome discipline, be gentle with yourself. You are a child of the universe no less than the trees and the stars; you have a right to be here.

And whether or not it is clear to you, no doubt the universe is unfolding as it should. Therefore be at peace with God, whatever you conceive Him to be. And whatever your labors and aspirations, in the noisy confusion of life, keep peace in your soul. With all its sham, drudgery and broken dreams, it is still a beautiful world. Be cheerful. Strive to be happy.

By Max Ehrmann

IF

If you can keep your head when all about you
Are losing theirs and blaming it on you,
If you can trust yourself when all men doubt you,
But make allowance for their doubting too;
If you can wait and not be tired by waiting,
Or being lied about, don't deal in lies,
Or being hated, don't give way to hating,
And yet don't look too good, nor talk too wise:

If you can dream - and not make dreams your master;
If you can think - and not make thoughts your aim;
If you can meet with Triumph and Disaster
And treat those two impostors just the same;
If you can bear to hear the truth you've spoken
Twisted by knaves to make a trap for fools,
Or watch the things you gave your life to, broken,
And stoop and build 'em up with worn-out tools:

If you can make one heap of all your winnings
And risk it on one turn of pitch-and-toss,
And lose, and start again at your beginnings
And never breathe a word about your loss;
If you can force your heart and nerve and sinew
To serve your turn long after they are gone,
And so hold on when there is nothing in you
Except the Will which says to them: 'Hold on!'

If you can talk with crowds and keep your virtue,
Or walk with Kings—nor lose the common touch,
If neither foes nor loving friends can hurt you,
If all men count with you, but none too much;
If you can fill the unforgiving minute
With sixty seconds' worth of distance run,
Yours is the Earth and everything that's in it,
And—which is more—you'll be a Man, my son!

Rudyard Kipling